Baby Animals in the Wild!

Squirrel Kits in the Wild

by Katie Chanez

Bullfrog Books

Ideas for Parents and Teachers

Bullfrog Books let children practice reading informational text at the earliest reading levels. Repetition, familiar words, and photo labels support early readers.

Before Reading

- Discuss the cover photo. What does it tell them?

- Look at the picture glossary together. Read and discuss the words.

Read the Book

- "Walk" through the book and look at the photos. Let the child ask questions. Point out the photo labels.

- Read the book to the child, or have him or her read independently.

After Reading

- Prompt the child to think more. Ask: Squirrel kits live in and around trees. How do their claws help them?

Bullfrog Books are published by Jump!
5357 Penn Avenue South
Minneapolis, MN 55419
www.jumplibrary.com

Library of Congress Cataloging-in-Publication Data

Names: Chanez, Katie, author.
Title: Squirrel kits in the wild / by Katie Chanez.
Description: Minneapolis, MN: Jump!, Inc., [2024]
Series: Baby animals in the wild! | Includes index.
Audience: Ages 5–8
Identifiers: LCCN 2022044301 (print)
LCCN 2022044302 (ebook)
ISBN 9798885244183 (hardcover)
ISBN 9798885244190 (paperback)
ISBN 9798885244206 (ebook)
Subjects: LCSH: Squirrels—Infancy—Juvenile literature.
Classification: LCC QL737.R68 C492 2024 (print)
LCC QL737.R68 (ebook)
DDC 599.3613/92—dc23/eng/20221003
LC record available at https://lccn.loc.gov/2022044301
LC ebook record available at https://lccn.loc.gov/2022044302

Editor: Eliza Leahy
Designer: Molly Ballanger

Photo Credits: Tei Sinthip/Shutterstock, cover (trunk); Nature Picture Library/SuperStock, cover (squirrels), 24; Jason L. Price/Shutterstock, 1; IrinaK/Shutterstock, 3 (top); itsjustluck/iStock, 3 (bottom); Sue Feldberg/Dreamstime, 4; Liz Bomford/Getty, 5, 23bm; Frank Lane Picture Agency/SuperStock, 6–7; Joe Blossom/Alamy, 8–9; Kassia Marie Ott/Shutterstock, 10–11; Jay Ondreicka/Shutterstock, 12, 23tm; Jessica Hartle/iStock, 13; Paul Smith/iStock, 14–15, 23tr; Nigel Harris/iStock, 16, 23tl; Glenn Mai/iStock, 17; AlecOwenEvans/iStock, 18–19; Ernie Janes/Alamy, 20–21; Nata.dobrovolskaya/Shutterstock, 21, 23bl; Robert Eastman/Shutterstock, 22; Chris Wetherell/Shutterstock, 23br.

Printed in the United States of America at Corporate Graphics in North Mankato, Minnesota.

Table of Contents

Fluffy Tails

A squirrel looks out.

Her nest is in this tree.

kit

Her kits are inside.

They are tiny.

The kits stay with Mom.

They drink her milk.

They grow fast!

fur

The kits stay warm
in the nest.

They grow fur.

Now they are six weeks old.

This one goes outside.

claw

It climbs trees.
Claws help.

It finds food.

It eats nuts and seeds.

Yum!

nut

tail

14

The kit grows.
Its tail gets fluffy!

It plays with other kits.

They chase each other.

They hide!

17

The kit grows up.
It finds a home in a tree.

It gathers food for winter.
Stay warm, squirrel!

nuts ····▶

Parts of a Squirrel Kit

What are the parts of a squirrel kit? Take a look!

ear

fur

tail

nose

leg

claw

paw

Picture Glossary

chase
To run after someone or something.

claws
Hard, sharp nails on the feet of some animals.

fluffy
Covered with soft, fine hair or fur.

gathers
Collects things in one place.

kits
Baby squirrels.

nest
A place built by an animal to live in and care for its young.

Index

To Learn More

FACT SURFER

Finding more information is as easy as 1, 2, 3.

❶ Go to www.factsurfer.com

❷ Enter "squirrelkits" into the search box.

❸ Choose your book to see a list of websites.